"If You Believe, You Can Achieve"

Visit the curious duo online:
www.mikeyandotis.com

Instagram - mikeyandotis

Copyright © 2019 by Mr. Ray Ray
Illustrations by Heather Workman

ISBN: 978-1-7331631-3-2 (hardback)
ISBN: 978-1-7331631-4-9 (paperback)
ISBN: 978-1-7331631-8-7 (e-book)

Published by Fun Family Publishing
www.funfamilypublishing.com

Mikey & otis
MOVE TO THE BURBS

By Mr. Ray Ray + His Friends

Otis was the first to open his eyes. He came out of his nestle to find his playpen fenced in with boxes and books.

He **OINKED**, "What is happening!?"

This woke up Mikey, who sprang from his bed.

"Oh no!" Mikey **WOOFED** from behind the pile of cardboard.
"We're moving out of the city today!"

Mom, overhearing Mikey and Otis, wanted to make them feel better. She told them about their new house with their own yard and an area filled with all kinds of animals.

Mom said, "Our growing family needs more space to have fun."

Mikey **WOOFED** and Otis **OINKED**, "More animals and more fun!"

They imagined all their new animal friends.

As the two brothers helped pack, they heard a loud HONK!

It was Dad, with a big moving van, Uncle Kim and Grandpa! The three of them started whisking boxes from the building to the van.

Mikey and Otis were excited about the move, but the playful brothers couldn't resist knocking over the boxes to help keep the family in the city a little while longer.

Otis and Mikey were enjoying playing until they heard a sneaky, "Meeooow!"

Mikey got ready to protect Otis again, when suddenly their neighborhood buddies appeared to wish The Boys goodbye and make sure they promised to visit them at the city park.

Seeing the dog pack, the pesky city cats ran off and meowed.

MAK 🌲 051
MAY

Dad hopped in the car and honked the horn to let Grandpa know he was ready to go.

The time to leave had come, so Mikey waved goodbye to the city.
Otis **OINKED**, "Smell ya later!"

And off they went, noses out the window, getting a last whiff of city air.

As they drove on, Mikey and Otis smelled something different out their windows.
A few moments later, Dad's moving van stopped at the new house.

CITY LIMITS

WELCOME
POP. 2017   647,805

Mikey and Otis couldn't believe their eyes! They jumped out of the car and ran all around the house and yard. Otis **OINKED** with glee and Mikey **WOOFED** with joy.

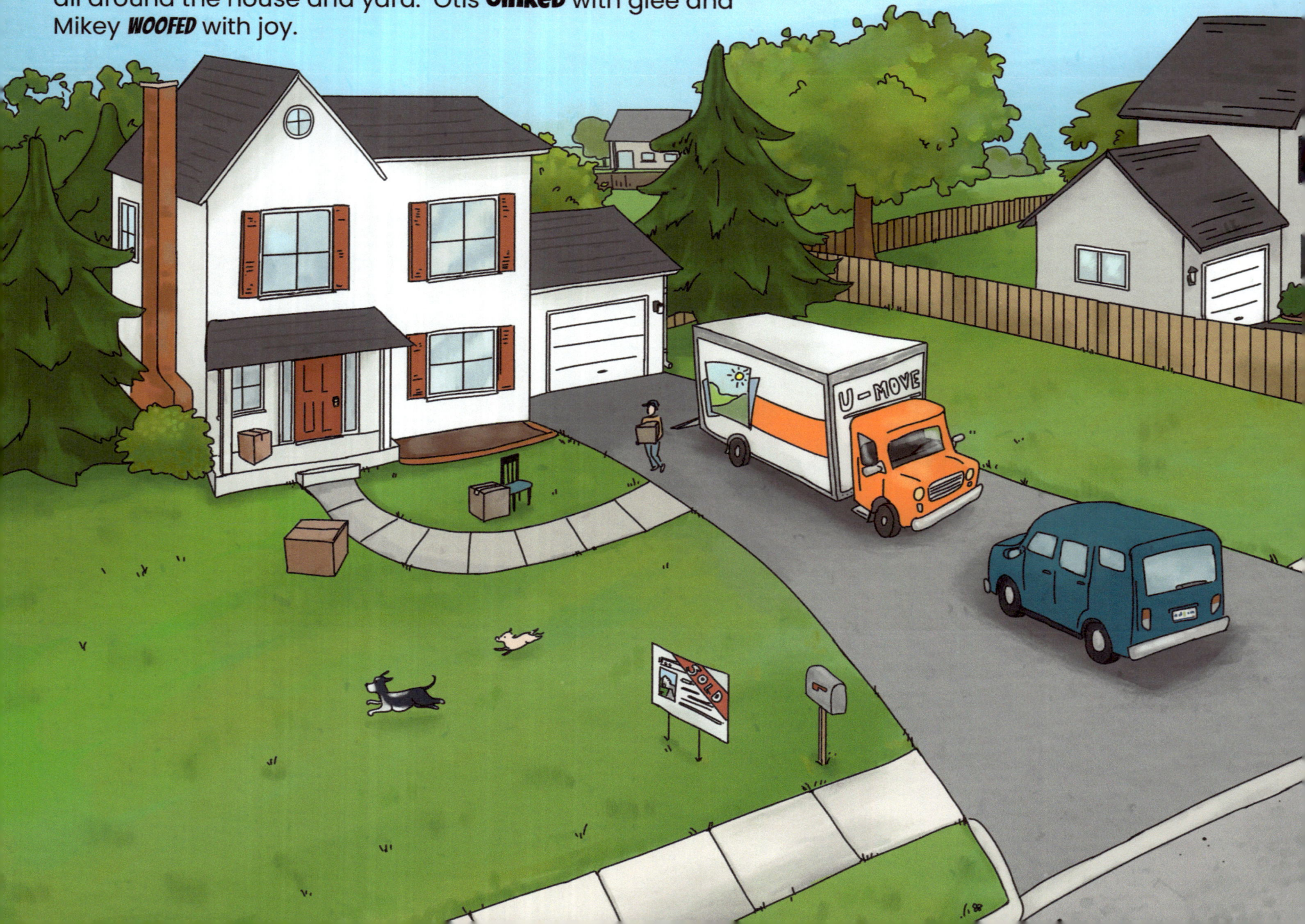

With so much space, Otis and Mikey got to pick their own rooms.
To everyone's surprise Mikey wanted to share a room with Otis because that's what best friends do.

After unpacking, Mikey and Otis wanted to take an adventure.

What they found made them even more excited! Mom had left a neighborhood map on the table. It showed all these parks, gardens, the little town village, and nature park.

Otis looked at Mikey and **OINKED**, "There's so much to explore, and I've never been to a nature park. We need to go now!"

Otis and Mikey raced outside to start their adventure.

They ran down the street and made it to the nature park on the edge of their neighborhood. They stopped for a moment and smiled at each other.

"This is so cool!" Mikey **WOOFED** as they ran on.

Distracted by the new exciting smells, they ran into and through the park.
They were now deep in the forest.

They kept running, exploring, and enjoying the forest.
The Boys were having such a great adventure!

As they explored the nature park, Mikey noticed a pair of eyes that were watching them. Not liking the look of the eyes, Mikey told Otis it was time to head back.

Otis agreed: "Mikey, do you have the map?"
They quickly realized they left it on the table. With a little hesitation,
Mikey **WOOFED**, "Follow me," and led the way, Otis galloping behind.

As they ran through the woods, a Big Bird flew overhead shadowing their every move.

And then, the big bird SCREECHED! The Boys ran. Little did they know they were going the wrong way! The big bird swooped down and tried to grab Otis!

Mikey busted a move and pushed Otis out of the way, both of them just barely escaping the bird's sharp claws.

The bird looped back into the sky and was coming in for a second attack, when suddenly behind Mikey and Otis, they heard a loud, "MEEEOOOOW!"

"Oh no!" thought The Boys. They were in real trouble!

Wait one second! Three cats went after the big bird. The cats kicked and meowed like ninjas. They scared the bird off for good.

The cats had come to the boys' rescue, just in time!

Mikey and Otis introduced themselves to these three new cat friends:
Coolio, Mario, and Zoe.

Their new friends let The Boys know they were going the wrong
direction and offered to get them back home.

On their way home, the group toured some of The Cool Cats' favorite spots: the park and town square.

By the time they got home, Mikey and Otis were thrilled with their new neightborhood! They made plans to play at the park and meet up at the local farmers' market in the town square.

Once inside, the scary bird was forgotten. Otis was so excited to tell Mom about his day and Mikey jumped into Dad's arms like nothing had happened.

"These two guys are getting along great!" said Dad.

NURSERY

"You're right!" replied Mom. "They must love their new home. Now, I wonder if they're ready for the next surprise..."